English Spanish Danish Dictionary

Simple everyday English
words and phrases
translated into
Spanish and Danish

Disclaimer: The content of this book is provided "as is" without any implied or explicit warranty of any kind.

English Spanish Danish Dictionary

to be	I want to be a doctor when I grow up.
ser - estar	Quiero ser médico cuando sea mayor.
at være	Jeg vil gerne være læge, når jeg bliver stor.
and	Sarah likes coffee, and John likes tea.
y	A Sarah le gusta el café y a John le gusta el té.
og	Sarah kan lide kaffe, og John kan lide te.
of	The book is the story of a young wizard.
de	El libro es la historia de un joven mago.
af	Bogen er historien om en ung troldmand.
in	I live in a small town near the mountains.
en	Vivo en un pequeño pueblo cerca de las montañas.
i	Jeg bor i en lille by tæt på bjergene.
to	She wants to go to the store to buy some groceries.
a	Quiere ir a la tienda a comprar algo de comida.
til	Hun vil gå i butikken for at købe nogle dagligvarer.

English Spanish Danish
Dictionary

to have	I need to have a cup of coffee in the morning.
tener	Necesito tomar una taza de café por la mañana.
har	Jeg skal have en kop kaffe om morgenen.

it	It's raining outside, so bring an umbrella.
eso	Afuera está lloviendo, así que trae un paraguas.
det	Det regner udenfor, så tag en paraply med.

I	I enjoy reading books in my free time.
yo	Disfruto leyendo libros en mi tiempo libre.
jeg	Jeg nyder at læse bøger i min fritid.

that	The movie that we watched last night was amazing.
ese	La película que vimos anoche fue increíble.
at	Den film, vi så i går aftes, var fantastisk.

for	I made this cake for your birthday.
para	Hice este pastel para tu cumpleaños.
til	Jeg lavede denne kage til din fødselsdag.

English Spanish Danish
Dictionary

you	Can you pass me the salt, please?
tú	¿Me puedes pasar la sal por favor?
du	Kan du give mig saltet, tak?
he	He is going to the gym after work.
él	Él va al gimnasio después del trabajo.
han	Han skal i fitnesscenter efter arbejde.
with	I'm having dinner with my family tonight.
con	Esta noche cenaré con mi familia.
med	Jeg spiser middag med min familie i aften.
on	I put the keys on the kitchen table.
en	Dejé las llaves sobre la mesa de la cocina.
på	Jeg lagde nøglerne på køkkenbordet.
to do	I have a lot of homework to do tonight.
hacer	Tengo mucha tarea que hacer esta noche.
at gøre	Jeg har mange lektier at lave i aften.

English Spanish Danish Dictionary

to say	She didn't know what to say during the meeting.
decir	Ella no supo qué decir durante la reunión.
at sige	Hun vidste ikke, hvad hun skulle sige under mødet.

this	This is my favorite book.
esta	Este es mi libro favorito.
dette	Dette er min yndlingsbog.

they	They are going to the beach this weekend.
ellos	Van a la playa este fin de semana.
de	De skal på stranden i weekenden.

at	I'll meet you at the park at 3 PM.
a	Te veré en el parque a las 3 p.m.
på	Jeg mødes i parken kl. 15.00.

but	I like pizza, but I also enjoy sushi.
pero	Me gusta la pizza, pero también disfruto el sushi.
men	Jeg kan godt lide pizza, men jeg nyder også sushi.

English Spanish Danish Dictionary

we	We are planning a trip to Europe next summer.
nosotros	Estamos planeando un viaje a Europa el próximo verano.
vi	Vi planlægger en tur til Europa næste sommer.
his	John forgot his wallet at home.
su	John olvidó su billetera en casa.
hans	John glemte sin pung derhjemme.
from	I received a postcard from my friend in Paris.
de	Recibí una postal de mi amigo en París.
fra	Jeg modtog et postkort fra min ven i Paris.
not	I'm not going to the party tonight.
no	No iré a la fiesta esta noche.
ikke	Jeg skal ikke til festen i aften.
by	The book was written by a famous author.
por	El libro fue escrito por un autor famoso.
ved	Bogen er skrevet af en berømt forfatter.

English Spanish Danish Dictionary

she	She is going to the concert with her friends.
ella	Ella va al concierto con sus amigos.
hun	Hun skal til koncert med sine venner.
or	Would you like tea or coffee for breakfast?
o	¿Quieres té o café para desayunar?
eller	Vil du have te eller kaffe til morgenmad?
as	He worked as a chef before becoming a teacher.
como	Trabajó como chef antes de convertirse en profesor.
som	Han arbejdede som kok, før han blev lærer.
what	What time is the movie starting?
qué	¿A qué hora empieza la película?
hvad	Hvad tid starter filmen?
to go	I want to go to the beach this weekend.
ir	Quiero ir a la playa este fin de semana.
at gå	Jeg vil på stranden i weekenden.

English Spanish Danish Dictionary

their	The Smiths are known for their beautiful garden.
su	Los Smith son conocidos por su hermoso jardín.
deres	The Smiths er kendt for deres smukke have.
to can	Can you pass me the salt, please?
poder	¿Me puedes pasar la sal por favor?
at kan	Kan du give mig saltet, tak?
who	Who is the new student in our class?
ese	¿Quién es el nuevo estudiante de nuestra clase?
hvem	Hvem er den nye elev i vores klasse?
to get	I need to get some groceries at the store.
llegar	Necesito hacer algunas compras en la tienda.
at få	Jeg skal have nogle dagligvarer i butikken.
if	If it rains, we'll have to reschedule the picnic.
si	Si llueve, tendremos que reprogramar el picnic.
hvis	Hvis det regner, bliver vi nødt til at omlægge picnicen.

English Spanish Danish Dictionary

would	Would you like a piece of cake?
haría	¿Quieres un pedazo de pastel?
ville	Vil du have et stykke kage?
her	I gave her a birthday present last week.
su	Le di un regalo de cumpleaños la semana pasada.
hende	Jeg gav hende en fødselsdagsgave i sidste uge.
all	All the students passed the exam.
todas	Todos los estudiantes aprobaron el examen.
alle	Alle elever bestod eksamen.
my	My cat is sleeping on the couch.
mi	Mi gato está durmiendo en el sofá.
min	Min kat sover på sofaen.
to make	I want to make a delicious homemade pizza.
hacer	Quiero hacer una deliciosa pizza casera.
at lave	Jeg vil lave en lækker hjemmelavet pizza.

English Spanish Danish
Dictionary

about	Tell me more about your trip to Paris.
acerca de	Cuéntame más sobre tu viaje a París.
om	Fortæl mig mere om din rejse til Paris.
to know	I don't know the answer to that question.
saber	No sé la respuesta a esa pregunta.
at vide	Jeg kender ikke svaret på det spørgsmål.
will	I will meet you at the restaurant at 7 PM.
será	Te veré en el restaurante a las 7 p.m.
vilje	Jeg møder dig i restauranten kl. 19.00.
up	Please pick up your toys from the floor.
arriba	Por favor recojan sus juguetes del suelo.
op	Saml venligst dit legetøj op fra gulvet.
one	I have one brother and two sisters.
uno	Tengo un hermano y dos hermanas.
en	Jeg har en bror og to søstre.

English Spanish Danish Dictionary

time	There's never enough time in a day.
hora	Nunca hay suficiente tiempo en un día.
tid	Der er aldrig tid nok på en dag.
there	There is a beautiful rainbow in the sky.
ahí	Hay un hermoso arco iris en el cielo.
der	Der er en smuk regnbue på himlen.
year	We celebrate our anniversary every year.
año	Celebramos nuestro aniversario cada año.
år	Vi fejrer vores jubilæum hvert år.
so	It's so hot outside; I need some ice cream.
entonces	Hace mucho calor afuera; Necesito un poco de helado.
så	Det er så varmt udenfor; Jeg skal bruge noget is.
to think	I often think about my future.
pensar	A menudo pienso en mi futuro.
at tænke	Jeg tænker ofte på min fremtid.

English Spanish Danish
Dictionary

when	When will you be arriving at the party?
cuando	¿Cuándo llegarás a la fiesta?
hvornår	Hvornår ankommer du til festen?

which	Which of these books do you want to read?
cual	¿Cuál de estos libros quieres leer?
hvilken	Hvilken af disse bøger vil du læse?

them	I gave them a gift for their anniversary.
ellos	Les di un regalo por su aniversario.
dem	Jeg gav dem en gave til deres jubilæum.

some	Can you pass me some sugar for my coffee?
algunos	¿Puedes pasarme un poco de azúcar para mi café?
nogle	Kan du give mig noget sukker til min kaffe?

me	She called me on the phone yesterday.
yo	Ella me llamó por teléfono ayer.
mig	Hun ringede til mig i går.

English Spanish Danish Dictionary

people	Many people enjoy going to the beach in the summer.
personas	Mucha gente disfruta yendo a la playa en verano.
mennesker	Mange mennesker nyder at gå til stranden om sommeren.
to take	Please remember to take your umbrella with you.
tomar	Por favor recuerda llevar tu paraguas contigo.
at tage	Husk at tage din paraply med.
out	Let's go out for dinner tonight.
fuera	Salgamos a cenar esta noche.
ud	Lad os gå ud og spise i aften.
into	We walked into the dark cave cautiously.
dentro	Entramos con cautela en la cueva oscura.
ind i	Vi gik forsigtigt ind i den mørke hule.
just	I'll be there in just a few minutes.
sólo	Estaré allí en unos minutos.
lige	Jeg er der om et par minutter.

English Spanish Danish
Dictionary

to see	I want to see the new movie at the theater.
ver	Quiero ver la nueva película en el cine.
at se	Jeg vil gerne se den nye film i teatret.
him	I saw him at the library yesterday.
él	Lo vi ayer en la biblioteca.
ham	Jeg så ham på biblioteket i går.
your	Is this your backpack on the chair?
tu	¿Es esta tu mochila en la silla?
jeres	Er det din rygsæk på stolen?
to come	When will you come to visit us?
venir	¿Cuándo vendrás a visitarnos?
at komme	Hvornår kommer du og besøger os?
could	Could you please pass the salt?
podría	¿Podrías pasar la sal?
kunne	Kan du venligst give saltet videre?

English Spanish Danish
Dictionary

now	I'm busy right now; can I call you back later?
ahora	Estoy ocupado en este momento; ¿Puedo llamarte más tarde?
nu	Jeg har travlt lige nu; kan jeg ringe tilbage senere?
like	I like to eat ice cream on hot days.
me gusta	Me gusta comer helado en los días calurosos.
synes godt om	Jeg kan godt lide at spise is på varme dage.
other	Are there any other options available?
otro	¿Hay otras opciones disponibles?
andet	Er der andre muligheder?
how	How do you bake a cake from scratch?
cómo	¿Cómo se hornea un pastel desde cero?
hvordan	Hvordan bager man en kage fra bunden?
then	We went to the park, and then we had lunch.
luego	Fuimos al parque y luego almorzamos.
derefter	Vi gik til parken, og så spiste vi frokost.

English Spanish Danish
Dictionary

its	The cat is washing its paws on the windowsill.
sus	El gato se lava las patas en el alféizar de la ventana.
dens	Katten vasker sine poter i vindueskarmen.
our	Our family is going on a vacation next week.
nuestro	Nuestra familia se irá de vacaciones la próxima semana.
vores	Vores familie tager på ferie i næste uge.
two	I have two dogs, a Labrador and a poodle.
dos	Tengo dos perros, un labrador y un caniche.
to	Jeg har to hunde, en labrador og en puddel.
more	Can I have some more cookies, please?
más	¿Puedo darme más galletas, por favor?
mere	Må jeg få nogle flere cookies, tak?
these	These shoes are too tight for me.
estas	Estos zapatos me quedan demasiado ajustados.
disse	Disse sko er for stramme til mig.

English Spanish Danish
Dictionary

to want	I want to go to the beach this weekend.
querer	Quiero ir a la playa este fin de semana.
at ville have	Jeg vil på stranden i weekenden.
way	There's always more than one way to solve a problem.
camino	Siempre hay más de una manera de resolver un problema.
vej	Der er altid mere end én måde at løse et problem på.
to look	She likes to look at the stars at night.
mirar	A ella le gusta mirar las estrellas por la noche.
at se	Hun kan lide at se på stjernerne om natten.
first	The race began, and I was the first to finish.
primero	La carrera comenzó y yo fui el primero en terminar.
først	Løbet begyndte, og jeg var den første, der kom i mål.
also	I love pizza, and I also enjoy sushi.
además	Me encanta la pizza y también disfruto el sushi.
også	Jeg elsker pizza, og jeg nyder også sushi.

English Spanish Danish
Dictionary

new	I got a new phone for my birthday.
nuevo	Recibí un teléfono nuevo para mi cumpleaños.
ny	Jeg fik en ny telefon til min fødselsdag.
because	We stayed home because it was raining outside.
porque	Nos quedamos en casa porque afuera estaba lloviendo.
fordi	Vi blev hjemme, fordi det regnede udenfor.
day	Sunday is my favorite day of the week.
día	El domingo es mi día favorito de la semana.
dag	Søndag er min yndlingsdag på ugen.
to use	Can I use your computer for a moment?
usar	¿Puedo usar tu computadora por un momento?
at bruge	Må jeg bruge din computer et øjeblik?
no	There is no milk left in the refrigerator.
no	No queda leche en el frigorífico.
ingen	Der er ingen mælk tilbage i køleskabet.

English Spanish Danish Dictionary

man	The man in the suit is the CEO of the company.
hombre	El hombre del traje es el director ejecutivo de la empresa.
mand	Manden i jakkesættet er virksomhedens administrerende direktør.

to find	I need to find my car keys.
encontrar	Necesito encontrar las llaves de mi auto.
at finde	Jeg skal finde mine bilnøgler.

here	I'm waiting for you here at the park.
aquí	Te espero aquí en el parque.
her	Jeg venter på dig her i parken.

thing	The most important thing is to be happy.
cosa	Lo más importante es ser feliz.
ting	Det vigtigste er at være glad.

to give	She decided to give her old clothes to charity.
dar	Decidió donar su ropa vieja a organizaciones benéficas.
at give	Hun besluttede at give sit gamle tøj til velgørenhed.

English Spanish Danish
Dictionary

many	There are many different types of flowers in the garden.
muchos	Hay muchos tipos diferentes de flores en el jardín.
mange	Der er mange forskellige typer blomster i haven.
well	I hope you feel well soon.
bien	Espero que te sientas bien pronto.
godt	Jeg håber du snart har det godt.
only	The store accepts cash only, no credit cards.
solamente	La tienda sólo acepta efectivo, no tarjetas de crédito.
kun	Butikken tager kun imod kontanter, ingen kreditkort.
those	Those shoes don't fit me properly.
aquellos	Esos zapatos no me quedan bien.
de der	De sko passer mig ikke ordentligt.
to tell	Can you tell me a story before bedtime?
decir	¿Puedes contarme un cuento antes de dormir?
at fortælle	Kan du fortælle mig en historie før sengetid?

English Spanish Danish
Dictionary

very	It's a very hot day in the summer.
muy	Es un día muy caluroso en verano.
meget	Det er en meget varm dag om sommeren.
even	He didn't believe me, even after I showed him the evidence.
incluso	No me creyó, incluso después de que le mostré las pruebas.
også selvom	Han troede mig ikke, selv efter at jeg viste ham beviserne.
back	I left my backpack at home by mistake.
espalda	Dejé mi mochila en casa por error.
tilbage	Jeg efterlod min rygsæk derhjemme ved en fejl.
any	Do you have any spare change for the parking meter?
alguna	¿Tienes algo de cambio para el parquímetro?
nogen	Har du noget ekstra skift til parkeringsmåleren?
good	She baked a delicious cake; it tastes really good.
bueno	Preparó un delicioso pastel; sabe muy bien.
godt	Hun bagte en lækker kage; det smager rigtig godt.

English Spanish Danish
Dictionary

woman	The woman in the red dress is my neighbor.
mujer	La mujer del vestido rojo es mi vecina.
kvinde	Kvinden i den røde kjole er min nabo.
through	We walked through the forest to reach the lake.
mediante	Caminamos por el bosque hasta llegar al lago.
igennem	Vi gik gennem skoven for at nå søen.
us	Can you pass the message to us?
nos	¿Puedes pasarnos el mensaje?
os	Kan du sende beskeden videre til os?
life	Life is full of surprises and challenges.
vida	La vida está llena de sorpresas y desafíos.
liv	Livet er fyldt med overraskelser og udfordringer.
child	My child loves to play at the park.
niño	A mi hijo le encanta jugar en el parque.
barn	Mit barn elsker at lege i parken.

English Spanish Danish
Dictionary

everyone	Everyone is welcome to the party.
todo el mundo	Todos son bienvenidos a la fiesta.
alle sammen	Alle er velkomne til festen.
to work	I have to work late tonight.
trabajar	Tengo que trabajar hasta tarde esta noche.
at arbejde	Jeg skal arbejde sent i aften.
down	Please put the book down on the table.
abajo	Por favor, deja el libro sobre la mesa.
ned	Læg venligst bogen på bordet.
to may	May I borrow your pen for a moment?
tener permiso	¿Puedo tomar prestado tu bolígrafo por un momento?
kan	Må jeg låne din kuglepen et øjeblik?
after	We'll have dinner after the movie.
después	Cenaremos después de la película.
efter	Vi spiser aftensmad efter filmen.

English Spanish Danish Dictionary

to should	You should study for the upcoming exam.
deberia	Deberías estudiar para el próximo examen.
at skulle	Du bør læse til den kommende eksamen.
to call	I will call you as soon as I get home.
llamar	Te llamaré tan pronto como llegue a casa.
at ringe	Jeg ringer til dig, så snart jeg kommer hjem.
world	Traveling allows you to see the world.
mundo	Viajar te permite ver el mundo.
verden	At rejse giver dig mulighed for at se verden.
over	The cat jumped over the fence.
encima	El gato saltó la valla.
over	Katten sprang over hegnet.
school	My sister goes to school every morning.
colegio	Mi hermana va a la escuela todas las mañanas.
skole	Min søster går i skole hver morgen.

English Spanish Danish
Dictionary

still	He is still waiting for his turn.
todavía	Todavía está esperando su turno.
stadig	Han venter stadig på sin tur.
to try	I want to try that new restaurant downtown.
intentar	Quiero probar ese nuevo restaurante del centro.
prøve	Jeg vil prøve den nye restaurant i centrum.
last	I saw you at the party last night.
último	Te vi en la fiesta anoche.
sidst	Jeg så dig til festen i går aftes.
to ask	Don't hesitate to ask if you have any questions.
preguntar	No dudes en preguntar si tienes alguna pregunta.
at spørge	Tøv ikke med at spørge, hvis du har spørgsmål.
to need	I need a new pair of shoes for the trip.
necesitar	Necesito un par de zapatos nuevos para el viaje.
at behøve	Jeg mangler et par nye sko til turen.

English Spanish Danish Dictionary

too	It's too hot outside to go for a run.
también	Hace demasiado calor afuera para salir a correr.
også	Det er for varmt udenfor til at løbe.
to feel	I feel happy when I'm with my friends.
sentir	Me siento feliz cuando estoy con mis amigos.
at føle	Jeg føler mig glad, når jeg er sammen med mine venner.
three	I have three siblings.
tres	Tengo tres hermanos.
tre	Jeg har tre søskende.
center	The hospital is located in the city center.
centrar	El hospital está ubicado en el centro de la ciudad.
centrum	Hospitalet ligger i byens centrum.
state	New York is a beautiful state to visit.
estado	Nueva York es un hermoso estado para visitar.
stat	New York er en smuk stat at besøge.

English Spanish Danish Dictionary

never	I never miss my morning coffee.
nunca	Nunca extraño mi café de la mañana.
aldrig	Jeg savner aldrig min morgenkaffe.
to become	She wants to become a doctor when she grows up.
convertirse	Quiere ser médico cuando sea mayor.
at blive	Hun vil gerne blive læge, når hun bliver stor.
between	The park is located between two tall buildings.
entre	El parque está ubicado entre dos edificios altos.
mellem	Parken ligger mellem to høje bygninger.
high	The mountain peak is very high.
alto	El pico de la montaña es muy alto.
høj	Bjergtoppen er meget høj.
really	I really enjoyed the concert last night.
de verdad	Realmente disfruté el concierto de anoche.
virkelig	Jeg nød virkelig koncerten i går aftes.

English Spanish Danish
Dictionary

something	Is there something you'd like to share with me?
alguna cosa	¿Hay algo que te gustaría compartir conmigo?
noget	Er der noget, du gerne vil dele med mig?

most	The library is the most peaceful place in town.
más	La biblioteca es el lugar más tranquilo de la ciudad.
mest	Biblioteket er det mest fredelige sted i byen.

another	Can I have another piece of cake
otro	¿Puedo tener otro pedazo de pastel?
en anden	Må jeg få et stykke kage til

much	There's so much work to do before the deadline.
mucho	Hay mucho trabajo por hacer antes de la fecha límite.
meget	Der er så meget arbejde at gøre inden deadline.

family	Family gatherings are always fun.
familia	Las reuniones familiares siempre son divertidas.
familie	Familiesammenkomster er altid sjove.

English Spanish Danish
Dictionary

own	She has her own business.
propio	Ella tiene su propio negocio.
egen	Hun har sin egen virksomhed.
to leave	I have to leave for the airport in an hour.
dejar	Tengo que salir para el aeropuerto en una hora.
at forlade	Jeg skal afsted til lufthavnen om en time.
to put	Please put the dishes in the dishwasher.
poner	Por favor, ponga los platos en el lavavajillas.
at sætte	Kom gerne opvasken i opvaskemaskinen.
old	My grandparents live in an old farmhouse.
antiguo	Mis abuelos viven en una antigua masía.
gammel	Mine bedsteforældre bor i en gammel bondegård.
while	I can read a book while waiting for my appointment.
mientras	Puedo leer un libro mientras espero mi cita.
mens	Jeg kan læse en bog, mens jeg venter på min aftale.

English Spanish Danish Dictionary

to mean	What does this word mean in Spanish?
significar	¿Qué significa esta palabra en español?
at mene	Hvad betyder dette ord på spansk?
to keep	It's important to keep your promises.
mantener	Es importante cumplir tus promesas.
at beholde	Det er vigtigt at holde dine løfter.
student	She is a dedicated student in her class.
estudiante	Ella es una estudiante dedicada en su clase.
studerende	Hun er en dedikeret elev i sin klasse.
why	Why did you choose this restaurant for dinner?
por qué	¿Por qué elegiste este restaurante para cenar?
hvorfor	Hvorfor valgte du denne restaurant til middag?
to let	Please let me know if you need any help.
dejar	Por favor, avíseme si necesita ayuda.
at lade	Lad mig det vide, hvis du har brug for hjælp.

English Spanish Danish Dictionary

great	The movie was great; I highly recommend it.
excelente	La película fue genial; Lo recomiendo altamente.
store	Filmen var fantastisk; Jeg anbefaler det stærkt.

same	We have the same taste in music.
mismo	Tenemos el mismo gusto musical.
samme	Vi har samme musiksmag.

big	That's a big house on the corner.
grande	Esa es una casa grande en la esquina.
stor	Det er et stort hus på hjørnet.

group	We are meeting with a group of friends tonight.
grupo	Esta noche nos reuniremos con un grupo de amigos.
gruppe	Vi mødes med en gruppe venner i aften.

to begin	Let's begin the meeting with an agenda review.
empezar	Comencemos la reunión con una revisión de la agenda.
at begynde	Lad os begynde mødet med en dagsorden-gennemgang.

English Spanish Danish
Dictionary

to seem	She seemed happy when she got the news.
al parecer	Parecía feliz cuando recibió la noticia.
at virke	Hun virkede glad, da hun fik nyheden.
country	Canada is a beautiful country to visit.
país	Canadá es un hermoso país para visitar.
land	Canada er et smukt land at besøge.
to help	Can you help me carry these groceries?
ayudar	¿Puedes ayudarme a llevar estos comestibles?
at hjælpe	Kan du hjælpe mig med at bære disse dagligvarer?
to talk	Let's sit down and talk about our plans.
hablar	Sentémonos y hablemos de nuestros planes.
at tale	Lad os sætte os ned og tale om vores planer.
where	Where is the nearest grocery store?
dónde	¿Dónde está la tienda de comestibles más cercana?
hvor	Hvor er den nærmeste købmand?

English Spanish Danish
Dictionary

to turn	Please turn off the lights before leaving.
girar	Por favor apague las luces antes de salir.
at dreje	Sluk venligst lyset, inden du tager af sted.

problem	Solving a math problem can be challenging.
problema	Resolver un problema matemático puede ser un desafío.
problem	At løse et matematisk problem kan være udfordrende.

every	I go for a walk every morning.
cada	Salgo a caminar todas las mañanas.
hver	Jeg går en tur hver morgen.

to start	I'll start working on the project tomorrow.
comenzar	Empezaré a trabajar en el proyecto mañana.
at begynde	Jeg begynder at arbejde på projektet i morgen.

hand	Please wash your hands before dinner.
mano	Lávese las manos antes de cenar.
hånd	Vask venligst dine hænder før aftensmaden.

English Spanish Danish
Dictionary

to might	It might rain later, so bring an umbrella.
poder	Puede que llueva más tarde, así que traiga un paraguas.
til måske	Det kan regne senere, så tag en paraply med.
deep	The ocean is incredibly deep and mysterious.
profundo	El océano es increíblemente profundo y misterioso.
dyb	Havet er utroligt dybt og mystisk.
to show	He will show you how to fix the issue.
mostrar	Él le mostrará cómo solucionar el problema.
at vise	Han vil vise dig, hvordan du løser problemet.
part	Being a part of the team is a great experience.
parte	Ser parte del equipo es una gran experiencia.
en del	At være en del af teamet er en stor oplevelse.
against	The soccer team played against their rivals.
en contra	El equipo de fútbol jugó contra sus rivales.
mod	Fodboldholdet spillede mod deres rivaler.

English Spanish Danish Dictionary

place	This cafe is a cozy place to relax.
sitio	Esta cafetería es un lugar acogedor para relajarse.
placere	Denne cafe er et hyggeligt sted at slappe af.
such	It's such a beautiful day to go for a walk.
tal	Es un día tan hermoso para salir a caminar.
sådan	Det er sådan en smuk dag at gå en tur.
again	I'll visit you again next month.
de nuevo	Te visitaré nuevamente el próximo mes.
en gang til	Jeg besøger dig igen næste måned.
few	I have a few friends coming to the party.
pocos	Tengo algunos amigos que vendrán a la fiesta.
få	Jeg har et par venner, der kommer til festen.
case	In case of rain, we'll move the picnic indoors.
caso	En caso de lluvia, trasladaremos el picnic al interior.
sag	I tilfælde af regn flytter vi picnicen indendørs.

English Spanish Danish
Dictionary

week	I have a busy week ahead at work.
semana	Tengo una semana ocupada por delante en el trabajo.
uge	Jeg har en travl uge forude på arbejdet.
company	My uncle works for a tech company.
empresa	Mi tío trabaja para una empresa de tecnología.
selskab	Min onkel arbejder for et teknologifirma.
system	The computer's operating system is outdated.
sistema	El sistema operativo de la computadora está desactualizado.
system	Computerens operativsystem er forældet.
each	Each student received a certificate.
cada	Cada estudiante recibió un certificado.
hver	Hver elev modtog et certifikat.
right	Please turn right at the traffic light.
derecha	Gire a la derecha en el semáforo.
højre	Drej til højre ved lyskrydset.

English Spanish Danish
Dictionary

program	The television program was very entertaining.
programa	El programa de televisión fue muy entretenido.
program	Tv-programmet var meget underholdende.
to hear	I can hear the birds singing outside.
escuchar	Puedo escuchar a los pájaros cantando afuera.
at høre	Jeg kan høre fuglene synge udenfor.
question	Do you have a question about the assignment?
pregunta	¿Tiene alguna pregunta sobre la tarea?
spørgsmål	Har du spørgsmål til opgaven?
during	I read a book during my lunch break.
durante	Leí un libro durante mi pausa para el almuerzo.
i løbet af	Jeg læste en bog i min frokostpause.
work	Hard work leads to success.
trabajo	El trabajo duro conduce al éxito.
arbejde	Hårdt arbejde fører til succes.

English Spanish Danish
Dictionary

to play	Children love to play at the playground.
jugar	A los niños les encanta jugar en el parque infantil.
at lege	Børn elsker at lege på legepladsen.
government	The government announced new policies.
gobierno	El gobierno anunció nuevas políticas.
regering	Regeringen annoncerede nye politikker.
to run	She can run faster than anyone in the race.
correr	Puede correr más rápido que nadie en la carrera.
at løbe	Hun kan løbe hurtigere end nogen anden i løbet.
small	I live in a small town in the countryside.
pequeña	Vivo en un pequeño pueblo en el campo.
lille	Jeg bor i en lille by på landet.
number	The phone number is listed on the website.
número	El número de teléfono aparece en el sitio web.
nummer	Telefonnummeret er angivet på hjemmesiden.

English Spanish Danish Dictionary

off	Please switch off your phone during the movie.
apagado	Por favor apague su teléfono durante la película.
af	Sluk venligst din telefon under filmen.
always	He is always punctual for meetings.
siempre	Siempre es puntual para las reuniones.
altid	Han er altid punktlig til møder.
to move	We need to move the furniture to the new house.
mover	Necesitamos trasladar los muebles a la nueva casa.
at flytte	Vi skal flytte møblerne til det nye hus.
to like	I like to have coffee in the morning.
gustar	Me gusta tomar café por la mañana.
at lide	Jeg kan godt lide at drikke kaffe om morgenen.
night	I enjoy stargazing at night.
noche	Disfruto contemplar las estrellas por la noche.
nat	Jeg nyder at kigge på stjernerne om natten.

English Spanish Danish Dictionary

to live	They live in a charming cottage by the lake.
vivir	Viven en una encantadora cabaña junto al lago.
at leve	De bor i et charmerende sommerhus ved søen.
Mr.	Mr. Smith is our new neighbor.
Señor	El Sr. Smith es nuestro nuevo vecino.
Hr	Mr. Smith er vores nye nabo.
point	The spaceship traveled to a distant point in space
punto	La nave espacial viajó a un punto distante en el espacio.
punkt	Rumskibet rejste til et fjernt punkt i rummet
to believe	I believe in working hard for success.
creer	Creo en trabajar duro para lograr el éxito.
at tro	Jeg tror på at arbejde hårdt for succes.
to hold	Please hold the door open for me.
sostener	Por favor, manténme la puerta abierta.
at holde	Hold venligst døren åben for mig.

English Spanish Danish
Dictionary

today	Today is a special day for our family.
hoy	Hoy es un día especial para nuestra familia.
i dag	I dag er en særlig dag for vores familie.
to bring	Can you bring a dessert to the party?
traer	¿Puedes traer un postre a la fiesta?
at bringe	Kan du tage en dessert med til festen?
to happen	Anything can happen in life.
suceder	Cualquier cosa puede pasar en la vida.
at ske	Alt kan ske i livet.
next	Our next meeting is scheduled for Tuesday.
siguiente	Nuestra próxima reunión está programada para el martes.
næste	Vores næste møde er planlagt til tirsdag.
without	I can't imagine life without my friends.
sin	No puedo imaginar la vida sin mis amigos.
uden	Jeg kan ikke forestille mig livet uden mine venner.

English Spanish Danish Dictionary

before	We should finish our work before the deadline.
antes de	Deberíamos terminar nuestro trabajo antes de la fecha límite.
før	Vi bør afslutte vores arbejde inden deadline.
large	The elephant is a large and majestic animal.
grande	El elefante es un animal grande y majestuoso.
stor	Elefanten er et stort og majestætisk dyr.
million	There are over a million stars in the night sky.
millón	Hay más de un millón de estrellas en el cielo nocturno.
million	Der er over en million stjerner på nattehimlen.
to must	You must complete your assignment by Friday.
deber	Debes completar tu tarea antes del viernes.
at måtte	Du skal færdiggøre din opgave senest fredag.
home	I love coming back to my cozy home.
hogar	Me encanta volver a mi acogedor hogar.
hjem	Jeg elsker at komme tilbage til mit hyggelige hjem.

English Spanish Danish Dictionary

under	The cat is hiding under the table.
debajo	El gato se esconde debajo de la mesa.
under	Katten gemmer sig under bordet.
water	I enjoy swimming in the clear blue water.
agua	Disfruto nadando en el agua azul clara.
vand	Jeg nyder at svømme i det klare blå vand.
room	We need to clean the living room.
habitación	Necesitamos limpiar la sala de estar.
værelse	Vi skal have gjort rent i stuen.
to write	I like to write poetry in my free time.
escribir	Me gusta escribir poesía en mi tiempo libre.
at skrive	Jeg kan godt lide at digte i min fritid.
mother	My mother makes the best homemade cookies.
madre	Mi madre hace las mejores galletas caseras.
mor	Min mor laver de bedste hjemmelavede småkager.

English Spanish Danish
Dictionary

area	This park is a beautiful area for picnics.
zona	Este parque es una hermosa zona para hacer picnics.
areal	Denne park er et smukt område til picnic.

national	The national flag represents our country.
nacional	La bandera nacional representa a nuestro país.
national	Nationalflaget repræsenterer vores land.

money	I need to save money for my vacation.
dinero	Necesito ahorrar dinero para mis vacaciones.
penge	Jeg skal spare penge til min ferie.

story	Tell me a story about your adventure.
historia	Cuéntame una historia sobre tu aventura.
historie	Fortæl mig en historie om dit eventyr.

young	The young girl is very talented in music.
joven	La joven tiene mucho talento para la música.
ung	Den unge pige er meget talentfuld inden for musik.

English Spanish Danish
Dictionary

fact	It's a fact that the Earth revolves around the Sun.
hecho	Es un hecho que la Tierra gira alrededor del Sol.
faktum	Det er et faktum, at Jorden kredser om Solen.

month	My birthday is next month.
mes	Mi cumpleaños es el mes que viene.
måned	Jeg har fødselsdag i næste måned.

different	Each snowflake is different from the other.
diferente	Cada copo de nieve es diferente del otro.
forskellige	Hver snefnug er forskellig fra den anden.

lot	There's a lot of traffic on the highway.
lote	Hay mucho tráfico en la autopista.
masse	Der er meget trafik på motorvejen.

study	I need to study for my upcoming exam.
estudiar	Necesito estudiar para mi próximo examen.
undersø-gelse	Jeg skal læse til min kommende eksamen.

English Spanish Danish
Dictionary

book	Reading a good book is my favorite pastime.
libro	Leer un buen libro es mi pasatiempo favorito.
bestil	At læse en god bog er min yndlingsbeskæftigelse.

eye	Her blue eyes are incredibly captivating.
ojo	Sus ojos azules son increíblemente cautivadores.
øje	Hendes blå øjne er utroligt fængslende.

job	Finding a job after college can be challenging.
trabajo	Encontrar un trabajo después de la universidad puede ser un desafío.
job	At finde et job efter college kan være udfordrende.

word	Please explain the meaning of this word.
palabra	Por favor explique el significado de esta palabra.
ord	Forklar venligst betydningen af dette ord.

though	I want to go for a walk, though it's raining.
aunque	Quiero salir a caminar, aunque está lloviendo.
selvom	Jeg vil gå en tur, selvom det regner.

English Spanish Danish
Dictionary

business	He runs a successful family business.
negocio	Dirige una exitosa empresa familiar.
forretning	Han driver en succesfuld familievirksomhed.

issue	The magazine covers a wide range of social issues.
problema	La revista cubre una amplia gama de temas sociales.
problem	Magasinet dækker en bred vifte af sociale emner.

side	The car was hit on the passenger side.
lado	El auto fue impactado del lado del pasajero.
side	Bilen blev ramt i passagersiden.

kind	She has a kind heart and helps others.
tipo	Tiene un corazón bondadoso y ayuda a los demás.
venlig	Hun har et venligt hjerte og hjælper andre.

four	There are four seasons in a year.
cuatro	Hay cuatro estaciones en un año.
fire	Der er fire årstider på et år.

English Spanish Danish
Dictionary

head	I have a headache; I need some rest.
cabeza	Me duele la cabeza; Necesito descansar.
hoved	Jeg har hovedpine; Jeg har brug for noget hvile.

far	The mountain is far from our current location.
lejos	La montaña está lejos de nuestra ubicación actual.
langt	Bjerget er langt fra vores nuværende placering.

black	The cat is completely black, except for its paws.
negro	El gato es completamente negro, a excepción de sus patas.
sort	Katten er helt sort, bortset fra dens poter.

long	The bridge is long and stretches over the river.
largo	El puente es largo y se extiende sobre el río.
lang	Broen er lang og strækker sig over floden.

both	Both of my parents are doctors.
ambos	Mis dos padres son médicos.
begge	Begge mine forældre er læger.

English Spanish Danish
Dictionary

little	My little sister loves to draw.
pequeño	A mi hermana pequeña le encanta dibujar.
lille	Min lillesøster elsker at tegne.

house	Their house has a beautiful garden.
casa	Su casa tiene un hermoso jardín.
hus	Deres hus har en smuk have.

yes	I said "yes" to the job offer.
si	Dije "sí" a la oferta de trabajo.
ja	Jeg sagde "ja" til jobtilbuddet.

since	I've known him since we were in kindergarten.
ya que	Lo conozco desde que estábamos en el jardín de infantes.
siden	Jeg har kendt ham siden vi var i børnehaven.

to provide	The organization provides food to the needy.
proveer	La organización proporciona alimentos a los necesitados.
at forsyne	Organisationen sørger for mad til trængende.

English Spanish Danish
Dictionary

service	The customer service at this restaurant is excellent.
servicio	El servicio al cliente en este restaurante es excelente.
service	Kundeservicen på denne restaurant er fremragende.
around	Let's walk around the park for some fresh air.
alrededor	Caminemos por el parque para tomar un poco de aire fresco.
rundt om	Lad os gå rundt i parken for at få lidt frisk luft.
friend	She's been my best friend for years.
amigo	Ella ha sido mi mejor amiga durante años.
ven	Hun har været min bedste ven i årevis.
important	Good health is very important in life.
importante	La buena salud es muy importante en la vida.
vigtig	Et godt helbred er meget vigtigt i livet.
father	My father is a talented musician.
padre	Mi padre es un músico talentoso.
far	Min far er en talentfuld musiker.

English Spanish Danish
Dictionary

to sit	Please sit down; the meeting is about to start.
sentarse	Por favor siéntate; La reunión está por comenzar.
at sidde	Sæt dig venligst ned; mødet er ved at starte.
away	He went away for a short vacation.
lejos	Se fue de vacaciones por unas cortas horas.
væk	Han tog afsted på en kort ferie.
until	I'll wait for you until you're ready to leave.
hasta	Te esperaré hasta que estés listo para partir.
indtil	Jeg venter på dig, indtil du er klar til at tage afsted.
power	The superhero has incredible power.
poder	El superhéroe tiene un poder increíble.
strøm	Superhelten har en utrolig kraft.
hour	The movie will start in an hour.
hora	La película empezará en una hora.
time	Filmen starter om en time.

English Spanish Danish
Dictionary

game	We're going to play a board game tonight.
juego	Esta noche vamos a jugar un juego de mesa.
spil	Vi skal spille et brætspil i aften.
often	I often go for a run in the morning.
a menudo	A menudo salgo a correr por la mañana.
tit	Jeg går ofte en tur om morgenen.
yet	I haven't seen her yet today.
todavía	Todavía no la he visto hoy.
endnu	Jeg har ikke set hende endnu i dag.
line	There was a long line at the movie theater.
línea	Había una larga cola en el cine.
linje	Der var lang kø i biografen.
political	The debate became highly political.
político	El debate se volvió altamente político.
politisk	Debatten blev højpolitisk.

English Spanish Danish Dictionary

end	The movie had a surprising twist at the end.
final	La película tuvo un giro sorprendente al final.
ende	Filmen havde et overraskende twist i slutningen.
among	He was among the first to arrive at the party.
entre	Fue uno de los primeros en llegar a la fiesta.
blandt	Han var blandt de første, der ankom til festen.
ever	Have you ever been to Paris?
nunca	¿Alguna vez has estado en París?
nogensinde	Har du nogensinde været i Paris?
to stand	She couldn't stand the hot weather.
pararse	No podía soportar el calor.
at stå	Hun kunne ikke holde ud i det varme vejr.
bad	Eating too much junk food is bad for your health.
malo	Comer demasiada comida chatarra es malo para la salud.
dårlig	At spise for meget junkfood er dårligt for dit helbred.

English Spanish Danish
Dictionary

to lose	I don't want to lose the game.
perder	No quiero perder el juego.
at tabe	Jeg vil ikke tabe spillet.
however	She tried her best; however, she didn't win.
sin embargo	Ella hizo lo mejor que pudo; sin embargo, ella no ganó.
imidlertid	Hun gjorde sit bedste; dog vandt hun ikke.
member	He's a member of the local club.
miembro	Es miembro del club local.
medlem	Han er medlem af den lokale klub.
to pay	Don't forget to pay the bill before leaving.
pagar	No olvides pagar la factura antes de partir.
at betale	Glem ikke at betale regningen inden afrejse.
law	Speeding is against the law.
ley	El exceso de velocidad es ilegal.
lov	Fremskyndelse er imod loven.

English Spanish Danish Dictionary

to meet	Let's meet for coffee tomorrow.
reunirse	Nos vemos mañana para tomar un café.
at møde	Lad os mødes til kaffe i morgen.
car	I just got a new car for my birthday.
coche	Acabo de recibir un auto nuevo para mi cumpleaños.
bil	Jeg har lige fået en ny bil til min fødselsdag.
city	New York City is known for its skyscrapers.
ciudad	La ciudad de Nueva York es conocida por sus rascacielos.
by	New York City er kendt for sine skyskrabere.
almost	I've almost finished reading this book.
casi	Ya casi termino de leer este libro.
næsten	Jeg er næsten færdig med at læse denne bog.
to include	The package should include all the items.
incluir	El paquete debe incluir todos los artículos.
at medtage	Pakken skal indeholde alle varerne.

English Spanish Danish
Dictionary

to continue	We'll continue the discussion in the next meeting.
continuar	Continuaremos la discusión en la próxima reunión.
at fortsætte	Vi fortsætter diskussionen på næste møde.
to set	Please set the table for dinner.
establecer	Por favor, prepara la mesa para la cena.
at sætte	Du bedes dække bord til middag.
later	We can discuss it later in the day.
luego	Podemos discutirlo más tarde en el día.
senere	Vi kan diskutere det senere på dagen.
community	Our community organized a charity event.
comunidad	Nuestra comunidad organizó un evento benéfico.
fællesskab	Vores samfund organiserede en velgørenhedsbegivenhed.
name	What's your name, please?
nombre	¿Cuál es tu nombre por favor?
navn	Hvad er dit navn, tak?

English Spanish Danish Dictionary

five	I have five apples in the basket.
cinco	Tengo cinco manzanas en la canasta.
fem	Jeg har fem æbler i kurven.
once	I visited that museum once when I was a child.
una vez	Visité ese museo una vez cuando era niño.
enkelt gang	Jeg besøgte det museum engang, da jeg var barn.
white	Her dress is a beautiful shade of white.
blanco	Su vestido es de un hermoso tono blanco.
hvid	Hendes kjole er en smuk nuance af hvid.
least	She tried her best, but it was the least she could do.
menos	Hizo lo mejor que pudo, pero era lo mínimo que podía hacer.
mindst	Hun prøvede sit bedste, men det var det mindste hun kunne gøre.
president	The President gave a speech on national television.
presidente	El presidente pronunció un discurso en la televisión nacional.
formand	Præsidenten holdt en tale på nationalt tv.

English Spanish Danish
Dictionary

to learn	It's never too late to learn something new.
aprender	Nunca es demasiado tarde para aprender algo nuevo.
at lære	Det er aldrig for sent at lære noget nyt.
real	The painting looks so real; it's incredible.
real	La pintura parece tan real; es increíble.
ægte	Maleriet ser så ægte ud; det er utroligt.
to change	I want to change the color of my room.
cambiar	Quiero cambiar el color de mi habitación.
at skifte	Jeg vil ændre farven på mit værelse.
team	Our team won the championship last year.
equipo	Nuestro equipo ganó el campeonato el año pasado.
hold	Vores hold vandt mesterskabet sidste år.
minute	I'll be back in a minute.
minuto	Regreso en un minuto.
minut	Jeg er tilbage om et øjeblik.

English Spanish Danish Dictionary

best	She's my best friend in the world.
mejor	Ella es mi mejor amiga en el mundo.
bedst	Hun er min bedste ven i verden.

several	We invited several friends to the party.
varios	Invitamos a varios amigos a la fiesta.
flere	Vi inviterede flere venner til festen.

idea	Do you have any idea for our next project?
idea	¿Tienes alguna idea para nuestro próximo proyecto?
ide	Har du en idé til vores næste projekt?

kid	The kids are playing in the park.
niño	Los niños están jugando en el parque.
barn	Børnene leger i parken.

body	Regular exercise is good for your body.
cuerpo	El ejercicio regular es bueno para tu cuerpo.
legeme	Regelmæssig motion er godt for din krop.

English Spanish Danish
Dictionary

nothing	There's nothing in the refrigerator.
nada	No hay nada en el frigorífico.
ikke noget	Der er intet i køleskabet.
ago	I saw her a year ago at the concert.
hace	La vi hace un año en el concierto.
siden	Jeg så hende for et år siden til koncerten.
to lead	He will lead the team to victory.
liderar	Llevará al equipo a la victoria.
at lede	Han vil føre holdet til sejr.
social	Social media has become very popular.
social	Las redes sociales se han vuelto muy populares.
social	Sociale medier er blevet meget populære.
to understand	I want to understand the meaning of this word.
comprender	Quiero entender el significado de esta palabra.
at forstå	Jeg vil gerne forstå betydningen af dette ord.

English Spanish Danish Dictionary

whether	I'm not sure whether I'll go to the party.
ya sea	No estoy seguro de si iré a la fiesta.
om	Jeg er ikke sikker på, om jeg vil tage til festen.
to watch	Let's watch a movie tonight.
ver	Veamos una película esta noche.
at se	Lad os se en film i aften.
together	We can achieve more when we work together.
juntos	Podemos lograr más cuando trabajamos juntos.
sammen	Vi kan opnå mere, når vi arbejder sammen.
to follow	Please follow the instructions carefully.
seguir	Por favor, siga las instrucciones cuidadosamente.
at følge	Følg venligst instruktionerne omhyggeligt.
matter	It's important to discuss this matter seriously.
material	Es importante discutir este asunto seriamente.
stof	Det er vigtigt at diskutere denne sag seriøst.

English Spanish Danish
Dictionary

parent	My parent is a teacher at the local school.
padre	Mi padre es profesor en la escuela local.
forælder	Min forælder er lærer på den lokale skole.

to stop	Please stop at the red traffic light.
detener	Por favor, deténgase en el semáforo en rojo.
at stoppe	Stop venligst ved det røde lyskryds.

face	I saw a familiar face at the store.
cara	Vi una cara familiar en la tienda.
ansigt	Jeg så et kendt ansigt i butikken.

anything	I'll do anything to make you smile.
cualquier cosa	Haré cualquier cosa para hacerte sonreír.
hvad som helst	Jeg vil gøre alt for at få dig til at smile.

to create	She can create beautiful art.
crear	Ella puede crear arte hermoso.
at skabe	Hun kan skabe smuk kunst.

English Spanish Danish Dictionary

public	The park is a public place for everyone.
público	El parque es un lugar público para todos.
offentlig	Parken er et offentligt sted for alle.
already	I've already finished my homework.
ya	Ya terminé mi tarea.
allerede	Jeg er allerede færdig med mine lektier.
to speak	She loves to speak in front of the class.
hablar	Le encanta hablar frente a la clase.
at tale	Hun elsker at tale foran klassen.
others	Let's consider the needs of others.
otros	Consideremos las necesidades de los demás.
andre	Lad os overveje andres behov.
to read	I like to read novels in my free time.
leer	Me gusta leer novelas en mi tiempo libre.
at læse	Jeg kan godt lide at læse romaner i min fritid.

English Spanish Danish Dictionary

level	The difficulty level of the game is high.
nivel	El nivel de dificultad del juego es alto.
niveau	Spillets sværhedsgrad er høj.
to allow	The teacher will allow us to use calculators.
permitir	El profesor nos permitirá utilizar calculadoras.
at tillade	Læreren vil tillade os at bruge lommeregnere.
to add	You can add sugar to your tea.
agregar	Puedes agregar azúcar a tu té.
at tilføje	Du kan tilføje sukker til din te.
office	He works in a busy office downtown.
oficina	Trabaja en una oficina muy concurrida en el centro.
kontor	Han arbejder på et travlt kontor i centrum.
to spend	We'll spend the weekend at the beach.
gastar	Pasaremos el fin de semana en la playa.
at bruge	Vi tilbringer weekenden på stranden.

English Spanish Danish
Dictionary

door	Please close the door behind you.
puerta	Por favor, cierra la puerta detrás de ti.
dør	Luk venligst døren bag dig.
health	Good health is essential for a happy life.
salud	La buena salud es esencial para una vida feliz.
sundhed	Et godt helbred er afgørende for et lykkeligt liv.
person	He's the kindest person I know.
persona	Es la persona más amable que conozco.
person	Han er den sødeste person, jeg kender.
art	She's a talented artist, known for her art.
arte	Es una artista talentosa, conocida por su arte.
kunst	Hun er en talentfuld kunstner, kendt for sin kunst.
sure	I'm sure we can find a solution.
por supuesto	Estoy seguro de que podemos encontrar una solución.
jo da	Jeg er sikker på, at vi kan finde en løsning.

English Spanish Danish
Dictionary

war	The war had a profound impact on the country.
guerra	La guerra tuvo un profundo impacto en el país.
krig	Krigen havde en dyb indvirkning på landet.
history	I love reading about history.
historia	Me encanta leer sobre historia.
historie	Jeg elsker at læse om historie.
party	We're hosting a party next weekend.
partido	Organizaremos una fiesta el próximo fin de semana.
parti	Vi holder en fest i næste weekend.
within	The answers are within the textbook.
dentro	Las respuestas están en el libro de texto.
inden for	Svarene findes i lærebogen.
to grow	Plants need sunlight to grow.
crecer	Las plantas necesitan luz solar para crecer.
at vokse	Planter har brug for sollys for at vokse.

English Spanish Danish
Dictionary

result	The exam result was excellent.
resultado	El resultado del examen fue excelente.
resultat	Eksamensresultatet var fremragende.
to open	Can you open the window, please?
abrir	¿Puede abrir la ventana por favor?
at åbne	Kan du åbne vinduet, tak?
change	Change is the only constant in life.
cambio	El cambio es la única constante en la vida.
lave om	Forandring er den eneste konstant i livet.
morning	I enjoy a quiet morning with coffee.
mañana	Disfruto de una mañana tranquila con un café.
morgen	Jeg nyder en stille morgen med kaffe.
to walk	Let's walk to the park together.
andar	Caminemos juntos al parque.
at gå	Lad os gå til parken sammen.

English Spanish Danish
Dictionary

reason	What's the reason behind your decision?
razón	¿Cuál es el motivo de su decisión?
grund	Hvad er årsagen til din beslutning?
low	The temperature is quite low in the winter.
bajo	La temperatura es bastante baja en invierno.
lav	Temperaturen er ret lav om vinteren.
to win	The team worked hard to win the championship.
ganar	El equipo trabajó duro para ganar el campeonato.
at vinde	Holdet arbejdede hårdt for at vinde mesterskabet.
research	He's conducting research in the lab.
investigación	Está realizando una investigación en el laboratorio.
forskning	Han forsker i laboratoriet.
girl	The little girl is playing in the garden.
niña	La niña está jugando en el jardín.
pige	Den lille pige leger i haven.

English Spanish Danish Dictionary

guy	That guy is always helpful and friendly.
chico	Ese chico siempre es servicial y amigable.
fyr	Den fyr er altid hjælpsom og venlig.
early	I woke up early to catch the sunrise.
temprano	Me levanté temprano para ver el amanecer.
tidlig	Jeg vågnede tidligt for at se solopgangen.
food	Italian food is my favorite cuisine.
comida	La comida italiana es mi cocina favorita.
mad	Italiensk mad er mit yndlingskøkken.
moment	This is a special moment in our lives.
momento	Este es un momento especial en nuestras vidas.
øjeblik	Dette er et særligt øjeblik i vores liv.
himself	He can fix the car by himself.
él mismo	Él mismo puede arreglar el auto.
ham selv	Han kan ordne bilen selv.

English Spanish Danish
Dictionary

air	The fresh mountain air is invigorating.
aire	El aire fresco de la montaña es tonificante.
luft	Den friske bjergluft er forfriskende.
teacher	Our math teacher is very patient.
profesor	Nuestro profesor de matemáticas es muy paciente.
lærer	Vores matematiklærer er meget tålmodig.
force	They used great force to open the door.
fuerza	Usaron mucha fuerza para abrir la puerta.
kraft	De brugte stor kraft på at åbne døren.
to offer	She'll offer assistance when needed.
ofrecer	Ella ofrecerá ayuda cuando sea necesario.
at tilbyde	Hun vil tilbyde hjælp, når det er nødvendigt.
enough	I have enough food for everyone.
suficiente	Tengo suficiente comida para todos.
nok	Jeg har mad nok til alle.

English Spanish Danish
Dictionary

education	Education is the key to success.
educación	La educación es la clave del éxito.
uddannelse	Uddannelse er nøglen til succes.

across	We walked across the bridge to get to the other side.
a través de	Cruzamos el puente para llegar al otro lado.
et kors	Vi gik over broen for at komme til den anden side.

although	Although it rained, we had a great picnic.
a pesar de que	Aunque llovió, hicimos un gran picnic.
selvom	Selvom det regnede, havde vi en fantastisk picnic.

to remember	I always remember our special moments.
recordar	Siempre recuerdo nuestros momentos especiales.
at huske	Jeg husker altid vores specielle øjeblikke.

foot	My foot got wet in the puddle.
pie	Mi pie se mojó en el charco.
fod	Min fod blev våd i vandpytten.

English Spanish Danish Dictionary

second	I'll be there in a second.
segundo	Estaré allí en un segundo.
sekund	Jeg er der om et øjeblik.
boy	The boy is playing with his toy truck.
chico	El niño juega con su camión de juguete.
dreng	Drengen leger med sin legetøjslastbil.
maybe	Maybe we should go to the beach tomorrow.
tal vez	Quizás deberíamos ir a la playa mañana.
måske	Måske skulle vi tage på stranden i morgen.
toward	We're heading toward the mountains.
hacia	Nos dirigimos hacia las montañas.
imod	Vi er på vej mod bjergene.
able	He is able to solve complex math problems.
poder	Es capaz de resolver problemas matemáticos complejos.
i stand	Han er i stand til at løse komplekse matematiske problemer.

English Spanish Danish
Dictionary

age	She celebrated her 30th birthday last week.
años	La semana pasada celebró su 30 cumpleaños.
alder	Hun fejrede sin 30 års fødselsdag i sidste uge.
policy	The company has a strict no-smoking policy.
política	La empresa tiene una estricta política de no fumar.
politik	Virksomheden har en streng ikke-ryger politik.
everything	She packed everything she needed for the trip.
todo	Empacó todo lo que necesitaba para el viaje.
alt	Hun pakkede alt, hvad hun skulle bruge til turen.
to love	I love spending time with my family.
amar	Me encanta pasar tiempo con mi familia.
at elske	Jeg elsker at tilbringe tid med min familie.
process	The cooking process takes time.
proceso	El proceso de cocción lleva tiempo.
behandle	Tilberedningsprocessen tager tid.

English Spanish Danish
Dictionary

music	I enjoy listening to classical music.
música	Disfruto escuchando música clásica.
musik	Jeg nyder at lytte til klassisk musik.
including	The menu offers a variety of dishes, including pasta.
incluso	El menú ofrece una variedad de platos, incluida la pasta.
inklusive	Menuen byder på en række retter, herunder pasta.
to consider	We need to consider all the options.
considerar	Necesitamos considerar todas las opciones.
at overveje	Vi skal overveje alle mulighederne.
to appear	The magician made a rabbit appear out of thin air.
a aparecer	El mago hizo aparecer un conejo de la nada.
vises	Tryllekunstneren fik en kanin til at dukke op ud af den blå luft.
actually	I'm not feeling well today, but I'll be fine, actually.
realmente	No me siento bien hoy, pero en realidad estaré bien.
rent faktisk	Jeg har det ikke godt i dag, men jeg har det faktisk godt.

English Spanish Danish Dictionary

to buy	I need to buy some groceries for dinner.
comprar	Necesito comprar algo de comida para la cena.
at købe	Jeg skal købe nogle dagligvarer til aftensmaden.
probably	He'll probably arrive late to the party.
probable-mente	Probablemente llegue tarde a la fiesta.
sandsyn-ligvis	Han kommer nok for sent til festen.
human	We are all part of the human race.
humano	Todos somos parte de la raza humana.
human	Vi er alle en del af den menneskelige race.
to wait	I'll wait for you at the cafe.
esperar	Te espero en el café.
at vente	Jeg venter på dig på cafeen.
to serve	She loves to serve her famous lasagna.
servir	Le encanta servir su famosa lasaña.
at tjene	Hun elsker at servere sin berømte lasagne.

English Spanish Danish
Dictionary

market	The farmers' market is open on Saturdays.
mercado	El mercado de agricultores está abierto los sábados.
marked	Bondemarkedet er åbent om lørdagen.
to die	We all hope for a peaceful way to die.
morir	Todos esperamos una forma pacífica de morir.
at dø	Vi håber alle på en fredelig måde at dø på.
to send	I'll send you the email shortly.
mandar	Te enviaré el correo electrónico en breve.
at sende	Jeg sender dig e-mailen snart.
to expect	What do you expect from the meeting?
esperar	¿Qué esperas del encuentro?
at forvente	Hvad forventer du af mødet?
couple	They make a great couple together.
pareja	Hacen una gran pareja juntos.
par	De udgør et fantastisk par sammen.

English Spanish Danish
Dictionary

sense	His sense of humor always makes me laugh.
sentido	Su sentido del humor siempre me hace reír.
følelse	Hans sans for humor får mig altid til at grine.
to build	They plan to build a new house next year.
construir	Planean construir una nueva casa el próximo año.
at bygge	De planlægger at bygge et nyt hus næste år.
to stay	I'll stay at the hotel for a week.
quedarse	Me quedaré en el hotel una semana.
at blive	Jeg bliver på hotellet i en uge.
to fall	The leaves will fall from the trees in the autumn.
caer	Las hojas caerán de los árboles en otoño.
at falde	Bladene vil falde fra træerne om efteråret.
nation	Our nation celebrates Independence Day.
nación	Nuestra nación celebra el Día de la Independencia.
nation	Vores nation fejrer uafhængighedsdag.

English Spanish Danish
Dictionary

plan	Let's discuss the plan for the weekend.
plan	Analicemos el plan para el fin de semana.
plan	Lad os diskutere planen for weekenden.

to cut	Can you help me cut these vegetables?
cortar	¿Puedes ayudarme a cortar estas verduras?
at klippe	Kan du hjælpe mig med at skære disse grøntsager?

college	She's studying at the local college.
universidad	Ella está estudiando en la universidad local.
kollegium	Hun studerer på det lokale college.

interest	His interest in art led him to become a painter.
interesar	Su interés por el arte lo llevó a convertirse en pintor.
interesse	Hans interesse for kunst førte til, at han blev maler.

death	The news of his death was very sad.
muerte	La noticia de su muerte fue muy triste.
død	Nyheden om hans død var meget trist.

English Spanish Danish Dictionary

course	I'm taking a cooking course next month.
curso	El mes que viene voy a hacer un curso de cocina.
rute	Jeg tager et madlavningskursus i næste måned.
someone	Someone is knocking at the door.
alguien	Alguien esta tocando la puerta.
nogen	Nogen banker på døren.
experience	Traveling is an enriching experience.
experiencia	Viajar es una experiencia enriquecedora.
erfaring	At rejse er en berigende oplevelse.
behind	He left his keys behind at the restaurant.
detrás	Dejó sus llaves en el restaurante.
bag	Han efterlod sine nøgler i restauranten.
to reach	We'll reach our destination in an hour.
alcanzar	Llegaremos a nuestro destino en una hora.
at nå	Vi når vores destination om en time.

English Spanish Danish
Dictionary

local	I like to support local businesses.
local	Me gusta apoyar a las empresas locales.
lokal	Jeg kan godt lide at støtte lokale virksomheder.
to kill	The hunter caught a fish, but he let it go.
matar	El cazador pescó un pez, pero lo soltó.
at dræbe	Jægeren fangede en fisk, men han slap den.
six	There are six apples in the basket.
seis	Hay seis manzanas en la canasta.
seks	Der er seks æbler i kurven.
to remain	The old castle will remain a historical site.
permanecer	El antiguo castillo seguirá siendo un sitio histórico.
at forblive	Det gamle slot forbliver et historisk sted.
effect	The medication had a positive effect on her health.
efecto	La medicación tuvo un efecto positivo en su salud.
effekt	Medicinen havde en positiv effekt på hendes helbred.

English Spanish Danish Dictionary

use	I can use this pen for writing.
utilizar	Puedo usar este bolígrafo para escribir.
brug	Jeg kan bruge denne pen til at skrive.
yeah	Yeah, I'll be at the party tonight.
si	Sí, estaré en la fiesta esta noche.
ja	Ja, jeg skal til festen i aften.
to suggest	She suggested going to the new restaurant.
sugerir	Ella sugirió ir al nuevo restaurante.
at foreslå	Hun foreslog at gå til den nye restaurant.
class	I'm taking a yoga class to relax.
clase	Estoy tomando una clase de yoga para relajarme.
klasse	Jeg tager en yogatime for at slappe af.
control	You need to have control over your emotions.
controlar	Necesitas tener control sobre tus emociones.
styring	Du skal have kontrol over dine følelser.

English Spanish Danish
Dictionary

to raise	They decided to raise funds for the charity.
elevar	Decidieron recaudar fondos para la organización benéfica.
at hæve	De besluttede at samle penge ind til velgørenheden.
care	She takes good care of her plants.
cuidado	Cuida muy bien sus plantas.
omsorg	Hun passer godt på sine planter.
perhaps	Perhaps we can go for a walk later.
quizás	Quizás podamos salir a caminar más tarde.
måske	Måske kan vi gå en tur senere.
late	I stayed up late to finish my project.
tarde	Me quedé despierto hasta tarde para terminar mi proyecto.
sent	Jeg blev sent oppe for at afslutte mit projekt.
hard	Working hard can lead to success.
difícil	Trabajar duro puede conducir al éxito.
svært	At arbejde hårdt kan føre til succes.

English Spanish Danish
Dictionary

field	He works in the field of medicine.
campo	Trabaja en el campo de la medicina.
mark	Han arbejder inden for medicin.
else	Is there anything else I can help you with?
más	¿Hay algo más en lo que pueda ayudarte?
andet	Er der andet jeg kan hjælpe dig med?
to pass	She studied hard to pass her exams.
pasar	Estudió mucho para aprobar sus exámenes.
at passere	Hun studerede hårdt for at bestå sine eksamener.
former	The former president visited our city.
ex	El expresidente visitó nuestra ciudad.
tidligere	Den tidligere præsident besøgte vores by.
to sell	They plan to sell their old furniture.
vender	Planean vender sus muebles viejos.
at sælge	De planlægger at sælge deres gamle møbler.

English Spanish Danish Dictionary

major	History is her major in college.
mayor	La historia es su especialidad en la universidad.
større	Historie er hendes hovedfag på college.
sometimes	Sometimes I like to go for a run.
algunas veces	A veces me gusta salir a correr.
sommetider	Nogle gange kan jeg godt lide at løbe.
to require	The job may require travel.
requerir	El trabajo puede requerir viajes.
at kræve	Jobbet kan kræve rejser.
along	Walk along the beach and enjoy the view.
a lo largo	Camine por la playa y disfrute de la vista.
hen ad	Gå langs stranden og nyd udsigten.
development	The city is undergoing rapid development.
desarrollo	La ciudad está experimentando un rápido desarrollo.
udvikling	Byen er i rivende udvikling.

English Spanish Danish
Dictionary

themselves	They built the house themselves.
sí mismos	Ellos mismos construyeron la casa.
dem selv	De byggede selv huset.

to report	He needs to report the incident to the police.
reportar	Necesita denunciar el incidente a la policía.
at rapport-ere	Han skal anmelde hændelsen til politiet.

role	Her role in the play was the lead character.
papel	Su papel en la obra fue el personaje principal.
rolle	Hendes rolle i stykket var hovedpersonen.

better	I hope you feel better soon.
mejor	Espero que pronto te sientas mejor.
bedre	God bedring.

economic	The economic situation is improving.
económico	La situación económica está mejorando.
økonomisk	Den økonomiske situation er i bedring.

English Spanish Danish
Dictionary

effort	Success requires hard work and effort.
esfuerzo	El éxito requiere trabajo duro y esfuerzo.
indsats	Succes kræver hårdt arbejde og indsats.
to decide	We need to decide on a restaurant for dinner.
decidir	Necesitamos decidirnos por un restaurante para cenar.
at afgøre	Vi skal beslutte os for en restaurant til middag.
rate	The interest rate on the loan is low.
tasa	La tasa de interés del préstamo es baja.
sats	Renten på lånet er lav.
strong	She is a strong advocate for environmental issues.
fuerte	Es una firme defensora de las cuestiones medio-ambientales.
stærk	Hun er en stærk fortaler for miljøspørgsmål.
possible	Anything is possible with determination.
posible	Todo es posible con determinación.
muligt	Alt er muligt med beslutsomhed.

English Spanish Danish Dictionary

heart	He has a kind heart and helps others.
corazón	Tiene un corazón bondadoso y ayuda a los demás.
hjerte	Han har et venligt hjerte og hjælper andre.
drug	The pharmacy provides various types of medicine.
droga	La farmacia ofrece varios tipos de medicamentos.
medicin	Apoteket leverer forskellige typer medicin.
show	The art show was a great success.
espectáculo	La exposición de arte fue un gran éxito.
at vise	Kunstudstillingen var en stor succes.
leader	He is a natural-born leader.
líder	Es un líder nato.
leder	Han er en naturligt født leder.
light	The morning light is beautiful.
ligero	La luz de la mañana es hermosa.
lys	Morgenlyset er smukt.

English Spanish Danish
Dictionary

voice	Her voice is soothing and melodious.
voz	Su voz es tranquilizadora y melodiosa.
stemme	Hendes stemme er beroligende og melodiøs.
wife	He's been married to his wife for 20 years.
esposa	Lleva 20 años casado con su esposa.
kone	Han har været gift med sin kone i 20 år.
whole	I ate the whole pizza by myself.
todo	Me comí toda la pizza yo solo.
hel	Jeg spiste hele pizzaen alene.
police	The police are here to help in emergencies.
policía	La policía está aquí para ayudar en emergencias.
politi	Politiet er her for at hjælpe i nødstilfælde.
mind	Can you read my mind and guess what I'm thinking?
mente	¿Puedes leer mi mente y adivinar lo que estoy pensando?
sind	Kan du læse mine tanker og gætte, hvad jeg tænker?

English Spanish Danish Dictionary

finally	I finally finished reading that book.
finalmente	Finalmente terminé de leer ese libro.
endelig	Jeg var endelig færdig med at læse den bog.
to pull	He needs to pull the rope to start the engine.
tirar	Necesita tirar de la cuerda para arrancar el motor.
at trække	Han skal trække i rebet for at starte motoren.
to return	I'll return your book after I'm done.
regresar	Te devolveré tu libro cuando haya terminado.
at vende tilbage	Jeg returnerer din bog, når jeg er færdig.
free	The concert tickets are free of charge.
gratis	Las entradas para el concierto son gratuitas.
ledig	Koncertbilletterne er gratis.
military	He served in the military for five years.
militar	Sirvió en el ejército durante cinco años.
militær	Han tjente i militæret i fem år.

English Spanish Danish
Dictionary

price	The price of the house is reasonable.
precio	El precio de la casa es razonable.
pris	Husets pris er rimelig.
report	She needs to submit her report by Friday.
reporte	Necesita presentar su informe antes del viernes.
rapport	Hun skal aflevere sin rapport senest fredag.
less	I have less work to do today.
menos	Tengo menos trabajo que hacer hoy.
mindre	Jeg har mindre arbejde at lave i dag.
according	According to the weather forecast, it'll rain tomorrow.
conforme	Según el pronóstico del tiempo, mañana lloverá.
ifølge	Ifølge vejrudsigten vil det regne i morgen.
decision	Making the right decision is crucial.
decisión	Tomar la decisión correcta es crucial.
afgørelse	At træffe den rigtige beslutning er afgørende.

English Spanish Danish Dictionary

to explain	Can you explain the concept to me again?
explicar	¿Puedes explicarme el concepto otra vez?
at forklare	Kan du forklare mig konceptet igen?
son	His son is studying abroad.
hijo	Su hijo está estudiando en el extranjero.
søn	Hans søn studerer i udlandet.
to hope	I hope for a peaceful world.
a la esperanza	Espero un mundo pacífico.
at håbe	Jeg håber på en fredelig verden.
to develop	The company plans to develop a new product.
desarrollar	La empresa planea desarrollar un nuevo producto.
at udvikle	Virksomheden planlægger at udvikle et nyt produkt.
view	The view from the mountain is breathtaking.
ver	La vista desde la montaña es impresionante.
udsigt	Udsigten fra bjerget er betagende.

English Spanish Danish
Dictionary

relationship	Their relationship has grown stronger over the years.
relación	Su relación se ha fortalecido con el paso de los años.
forhold	Deres forhold er blevet stærkere gennem årene.
to carry	Can you carry these bags for me, please?
llevar	¿Puedes llevarme estas bolsas, por favor?
at bære	Kan du bære disse tasker for mig, tak?
town	I live in a small town in the countryside.
pueblo	Vivo en un pequeño pueblo en el campo.
by	Jeg bor i en lille by på landet.
road	The road to the beach is scenic and beautiful.
la carretera	El camino a la playa es pintoresco y hermoso.
vej	Vejen til stranden er naturskøn og smuk.
to drive	I'll drive you to the airport tomorrow.
conducir	Te llevaré al aeropuerto mañana.
at køre	Jeg kører dig til lufthavnen i morgen.

English Spanish Danish
Dictionary

arm	He injured his arm while playing soccer.
brazo	Se lastimó el brazo mientras jugaba fútbol.
arm	Han sårede sin arm, mens han spillede fodbold.
to break	Be careful not to break the glass.
romper	Tenga cuidado de no romper el cristal.
at ødelægge	Pas på ikke at knuse glasset.
difference	There's a big difference between the two options.
diferencia	Hay una gran diferencia entre las dos opciones.
forskel	Der er stor forskel på de to muligheder.
to thank	I want to thank you for your help.
agradecer	Quiero agradecerte por tu ayuda.
at takke	Jeg vil gerne takke dig for din hjælp.
to receive	She will receive a gift for her birthday.
recibir	Recibirá un regalo por su cumpleaños.
at modtage	Hun får en gave til sin fødselsdag.

English Spanish Danish
Dictionary

value	Honesty is a value I cherish.
valor	La honestidad es un valor que aprecio.
værdi	Ærlighed er en værdi, jeg værdsætter.
building	The tallest building in the city is impressive.
edificio	El edificio más alto de la ciudad es impresionante.
bygning	Den højeste bygning i byen er imponerende.
action	It's time for action, not just words.
acción	Es hora de actuar, no sólo de palabras.
handling	Det er tid til handling, ikke kun ord.
full	The restaurant was full of customers.
completo	El restaurante estaba lleno de clientes.
fuld	Restauranten var fuld af kunder.
to join	I'd like to join the hiking club.
unir	Me gustaría unirme al club de senderismo.
at deltage	Jeg vil gerne være med i vandreklubben.

English Spanish Danish
Dictionary

season	Winter is my favorite season.
temporada	El invierno es mi estación favorita.
sæson	Vinteren er min yndlingsårstid.

society	Our society is becoming more diverse.
sociedad	Nuestra sociedad es cada vez más diversa.
samfund	Vores samfund bliver mere mangfoldigt.

because	I'm staying home because of the rain.
porque	Me quedo en casa por la lluvia.
fordi	Jeg bliver hjemme på grund af regnen.

tax	Don't forget to pay your income tax.
impuesto	No olvides pagar tu impuesto sobre la renta.
skat	Glem ikke at betale din indkomstskat.

director	The director of the company is making changes.
director	El director de la empresa está haciendo cambios.
direktør	Direktøren for virksomheden foretager ændringer.

English Spanish Danish
Dictionary

position	She secured a high position in the company.
posición	Consiguió un alto puesto en la empresa.
position	Hun sikrede sig en høj position i virksomheden.

player	He is a talented soccer player.
jugador	Es un futbolista talentoso.
spiller	Han er en talentfuld fodboldspiller.

to agree	I agree with your point of view.
llegar a un acuerdo	Estoy de acuerdo con su punto de vista.
at blive enige	Jeg er enig i dit synspunkt.

especially	I love traveling, especially to new places.
especialmente	Me encanta viajar, especialmente a lugares nuevos.
især	Jeg elsker at rejse, især til nye steder.

record	He broke a world record in swimming.
grabar	Rompió un récord mundial en natación.
optage	Han slog verdensrekord i svømning.

English Spanish Danish
Dictionary

to pick	Please pick up some groceries on your way home.
recoger	Por favor, recoja algunos alimentos de camino a casa.
at vælge	Hent venligst nogle dagligvarer på vej hjem.
to wear	She likes to wear colorful dresses.
usar	A ella le gusta usar vestidos coloridos.
at have på	Hun kan godt lide at gå i farverige kjoler.
paper	I need to buy some printer paper.
papel	Necesito comprar papel para impresora.
papir	Jeg skal købe noget printerpapir.
special	Today is a special day, let's celebrate.
especial	Hoy es un día especial, celebremos.
særlig	I dag er en speciel dag, lad os fejre det.
space	There's not enough space in the garage.
espacio	No hay suficiente espacio en el garaje.
plads	Der er ikke plads nok i garagen.

English Spanish Danish
Dictionary

ground	The children play on the school ground.
suelo	Los niños juegan en el terreno de la escuela.
jord	Børnene leger på skolens grund.
to support	We should support local businesses.
apoyar	Deberíamos apoyar a las empresas locales.
at støtte	Vi bør støtte lokale virksomheder.
event	The annual festival is a grand event.
evento	El festival anual es un gran evento.
begivenhed	Den årlige festival er en storslået begivenhed.
whose	Whose phone is this on the table?
cuyo	¿De quién es este teléfono sobre la mesa?
hvis	Hvis telefon er dette på bordet?
site	The construction site is busy with workers.
sitio	El sitio de construcción está ocupado con trabajadores.
websted	Byggepladsen er travl med arbejdere.

English Spanish Danish
Dictionary

to end	I hope this argument will end soon.
terminar	Espero que esta discusión termine pronto.
at afslutte	Jeg håber, at dette argument snart vil ende.
project	The new project is challenging but exciting.
proyecto	El nuevo proyecto es desafiante pero emocionante.
projekt	Det nye projekt er udfordrende, men spændende.
to hit	The baseball player hit a home run.
golpear	El beisbolista conectó un jonrón.
at ramme	Baseballspilleren slog et hjem.
to base	We should base our decision on facts.
a la base	Deberíamos basar nuestra decisión en hechos.
at basere	Vi bør basere vores beslutning på fakta.
activity	The after-school activity is a dance class.
actividad	La actividad extraescolar es una clase de baile.
aktivitet	Efterskoleaktiviteten er en dansetime.

English Spanish Danish
Dictionary

star	She's a rising star in the music industry.
estrella	Ella es una estrella en ascenso en la industria de la música.
stjerne	Hun er en stigende stjerne i musikindustrien.

table	Please set the table for dinner.
mesa	Por favor, prepara la mesa para la cena.
bord	Du bedes dække bord til middag.

need	I need some help with this task.
necesitar	Necesito ayuda con esta tarea.
brug for	Jeg har brug for hjælp til denne opgave.

court	They are going to court over a property dispute.
corte	Van a los tribunales por una disputa de propiedad.
ret	De går i retten i en ejendomsstrid.

to produce	The factory will produce more cars.
producir	La fábrica producirá más coches.
at producere	Fabrikken vil producere flere biler.

English Spanish Danish
Dictionary

to eat	Let's eat at the new restaurant in town.
comer	Comamos en el nuevo restaurante de la ciudad.
at spise	Lad os spise på den nye restaurant i byen.
to teach	She loves to teach art to children.
enseñar	Le encanta enseñar arte a los niños.
at lære	Hun elsker at undervise børn i kunst.
oil	We need to change the oil in the car.
petróleo	Necesitamos cambiar el aceite del coche.
olie	Vi skal skifte olie i bilen.
half	I'll take half of the pizza, and you can have the other half.
medio	Yo tomaré la mitad de la pizza y tú puedes quedarte con la otra mitad.
halvt	Jeg tager halvdelen af pizzaen, og du kan få den anden halvdel.
situation	The current situation is quite complex.
situación	La situación actual es bastante compleja.
situation	Den nuværende situation er ret kompleks.